The Traveller

Part I

by Mateen Manek

Published by The Scribe's Theatre Company

ISBN: 978-0-9940824-2-8

Cover Art by Hasanain Rashid of Flying Rashid Productions

http://theclearlyilliteratecafe.com
mateen@theclearlyilliteratecafe.com

Introduction

I went to the store and bought a bunch of notebooks.
They were small, almost the size of a wallet. I took one
and carried it in my pocket, taking it with me wherever
I went.

I write a lot of poetry when I'm not at home, typically
inspired by things that surround me on my journeys.
Sometimes I don't have anything to write on, so I have
to remember my thoughts until I get home. That never
worked.

The poems you are about to read are those poems
that were written in the notebook, on my phone, or in
my memory. These are poems inspired by my
journeys, some of which were to new places and
others to places I had been to very often. This is a
very different collection from my other poems, and
many of my poems have been rejected from this
compilation. You might also notice that some of these
are stories rather than poems. The pieces are
presented in one continuous flow and are not given
titles, because that's how most of them were written.
The three stars separated one moment from another.

This is why the book is called _The Traveller_. While
reading these, some of these poems painted vivid
moments that I have lived through, and almost serve

as textual photographs. These poems are like memories of my travels and my journeys, and now they travel to you. My favourite poems have managed to do that for me, and sometimes even my favourite stories. My poems might not have that effect for you, but I can only hope you leave this book gaining something.

I really appreciate you taking the time to read the introduction, which is usually the part of the book I would skip. I just thought I would leave you with some thoughts before you began the actual poems. Thank you for taking your time for this book. I've found something amazing in poetry and have always loved to share my work. I pray that you appreciate it.

Poems

***

Still and serene, shimmering shimmer;
A never-ending path to a world I
cannot see
I might take this road, set sail on a
journey,
And as I go, study the reflection I see
in the sea.

But I know there must be an end-
A place I might leave my boat and
walk away.
And once I reach the shore, I hope to
be ready
For a new journey to start again.

And I find the surface, as far as it may
be.
There is still land underneath where I
will rest my feet.
But I soar above, caught by the
reflection in the sea;
I know that, in my hands, I would never
drop me.

I have no paddle or motor
Nothing or no one to act as a guide.
I have me to follow;
I have myself and I have I.

***

I look upon the sea, and find myself
staring back at the reflection.
Although it is not me, it is a different
self;
One with newer books on a newer
shelf,
One on a road with no map to be
bound by.

In the sea I find fish to catch,
Ones that I had not look for so many
years ago.

I will take upon the sea.
I will find my reflection and take upon
it,
Wearing it like a coat of armor.
I will become the man I had seen when
I was at shore.

I want to return as the man of the sea.
I want to look at my reflection,
I want to see me.

***

I would become nothing
To see a smile like hers.

***

I could sit here all night
And let the rain wash my face.
The mist that dances upon my skin
Feels like a fresh start.

***

Sometimes we prefer
To pick at the scabs
Rather than let it heal.

***

There she is.
I've found her shadow
In the corner of my eye,
As the minty air floats through the
evening sky.
As I turn my head to find her,
She is gone.
She is long gone.

And so I wait;
Same time on the same day,
Hoping to correct my past mistake.
I've found her only in writing,
And in the ghostly image my mind
creates.

And all that comes to mind is the
sound of her voice
As I walk through the minty air garden
After a glorious rainfall.
And though the day has darkened,
It has never looked so beautiful.

***

She was the moon
And I were the sun,
But I had never imagined
How it was to be on the other side of
the world.

And I've heard fables;
Whispers that stars left behind.
I have shone light on the desks of
poets
As they write lines of her,
Inspired by the restless nights
Of memorizing every fine detail of her
being.

I wish I were these poets
That had the chance to meet her and
meet her again.
But I only see my days in one way
And my presence lies in her absence.

But years from now we shall meet;
Face to face, closer than any being
could be.
I still feel my hand wrapped around her
waist
Pulling her closer as if the hour never
met its end.
And though our love may last a brief
moment,

It is enough to soothe my restless
heart.

As years and years filled with
emptiness go by
Those moments of love will remain in
the night.

So we shall turn, and turn, and turn
Until we finally meet on that rare night;
Our meeting famed, our shadow one,
As our dance eclipses over the
unearthly sky.

She was the moon
And I were the sun,
But I have never imaged
How it was to be on the other side of
the world.

***

Sing me your song
And put me in a trance
Of love and devotion.
Your song blows on the embers
Of my soul and awakens them
From its dormant state.

Sing me your song
So I can fall in love.
Sing me your song
So I may discover my fire.
Sing me your song
And, someday, I will also sing along.

***

She was a dragon,
But her fiery tongue soothed me
And awoke the beast buried
Deep within my soul.
I have never met a beast
As beastly as me,
Our fires battle each other
Until they become one.
They always become one.

***

It may seem like I do things for my
ego,
When, in fact, I do it for your attention.
And though there might be a million
eyes on me,
Yours are the only ones I'd look for.

***

Our conversations
Are a blank canvas
That should be filled
With different colours,
And different textures,
And be void of space.

But it is not so, nor can ever be.

***

I love to splash cold water on my face
Because in every drop lies a
substance
That invades my body and swims
down,
Finding every cell and releasing
The sweetest, most peaceful piece of
purity,
And, for a moment, brings me
To a point of total energy.

***

As my son sleeps in his
beige-coloured crib
I hear another child's screams vividly
in my ear.
I know that he is distant, but I can feel
Her cries penetrate my chest.
I don't know that sound but it sounds
like blood,
Something that I am lucky to never
know.

I think of my son and the pain of this
child,
Wishing that he would never meet an
ounce of that world.
For my heart would die if I had ever
heard
The screams from him that I had heard
from her.

***

There is such wonder in the light
shining over these towns.
It's so majestic and inspiring.
It's a restart, or a brand new
beginning.
A reminder of another day.
A reminder that the world is yours.

***

I followed her,
And she took me to your doorstep
And taught me love.

I carry her poems in my pocket
And read them before I dream.
In her sleep she thinks of you
And I wish I could say the same.

We don't speak the same,
But we had loved the same one in the
same way.
I've finally found you through her,
And now I've come to learn
That you helped her find me.

As I look over the rooftops,
At the earliest point of this morning,
I see the sun rising.
I hear the birds singing.
I feel her love beaming.

I am closer to you.

***

Each blade of grass
Is a fact of your true might.
Even the invisible
Is a miracle.

***

In my room, it is dark.
My eyes grow heavy.
And as I stand in weakness,
I hear a bird singing outside my
window.
There's something in that
That makes my eyes stronger
And makes me want to keep going.

***

The clock struck twelve, and I ran.
I don't know what possessed me to
find myself at her door at this hour, but
it seemed right. There she was,
wearing a white dress that draped, and
a pair of heels that didn't seem to hurt
her feet. She was carrying them,
clutching onto them as if to keep them
safe. She then asked me to go on a
walk, which seemed like an odd
request given her attire. I asked her if
she needed something to wear on her
feet, and she raised her heels in an
obvious tone. I finally agreed; a walk
with her in the empty moonlit street
was what I had dreamt of this past life.
I took nothing- I didn't expect to come
back.

***

Crescent, reddish rock
Descending onto the surface of the
earth.
Following me, becoming my
destination.
A fixed point that will always be too far
But it's something magical in sight-
It's unreal.

It looks as if it has a face-
A sleeping face, mind you, but one
That looks in comfort, cradled by the
air
And sleeping amongst the stars.

I've never seen it red, though
I've imagined it blue.
Maybe because that's the colour
That filled the walls of my room.

***

Our heart knows the words
But our mind intercedes,
Coming up with reasons
Why you shouldn't speak.

Ignore her, ignore her.
Let your heart run loose.
Your mind has been drawing plans
That will show only when you lose.

***

Even mosquitos hover to the light
As if they can't stand the darkness,
And so do the shadows
Of the taller things.

But we must confront our demons.
Listen to the songs of our past,
(The ones that produce those vile
images)
And sing along; hoping to burn
The pages from that book
And finally move on.

Eventually the lights will go out-
That will finally catch your attention.
When the burning embers slowly
darken.
You wonder if maybe you should be
out here,
But soon you'll realize
The lights are meant to come back on;
They only stay out for a brief moment.

***

Her eyes shimmer
Like diamonds held to the sun.
They remind me of stars
On a cloudy eve
Breaking through and shining;
Finding me,
Telling me to come closer.

And that's what I remember so vividly;
The wonder-filled look in your eye
Followed by that smile, and the
wrinkles near your eyes that would
follow;
And suddenly, the images came to life.

***

I've told people that I've seen the smile
of an angel
And they look at me as if I was mad.

They have not caught a glimpse of
your eye,
Otherwise they would be mad too.

***

The air reminds me of a foreign home
Far and far away,
Past the mountains and the lakes and
the oceans.

A home filled both with misery and
content;
A style that was impossible to mimic.
And one, stubborn for sure, but an
angel nonetheless
Once you look past the flaws and
beyond the surface.
One that I had found on the journey
home,
Because we only notice what is
missing
And not what is already there.

I hope I find myself back there in time,
And not knocking on the door
Only to find out that that are no longer
in.

***

The future is never certain;
It is filled with so many things.
Picture the sky and the stars behind it
And see if you could count them all-
Even the ones you could not see.
That is telling the future;
Looking at a map that goes on forever,
Giving you a picture but never a
scene.
Sometimes not knowing is like pins on
your nerves.
Sometimes not knowing is so serene.

But I'm afraid to go on
I look at the sky and see only dark
clouds.
It might be raining soon,
Or the sun might appear.
But who knows?
I certainly don't.

***

We lost time,
Even though she stood there
Looking at us,
Curious about us.
In the process of finding her
We lost ourselves
We split back into two entities
And once again became strangers.
They continued looking on
As we tried to find her.
She told me she saw us
And told me that we were too busy
Finding ourselves.

***

I can count the many moments--
The countless memories in which
I should have told you
How you are the fire on a cold winter
day,
Or how you act as the wind to my
humid heart.
Your words become the mist that
breathes over my charred soul.
The coal becomes a diamond,
And you are the force that made it so.

And I have letters writ,
With your address written,
Sitting atop my mailbox.
But every time I go near it
I leave it alone,
Singing the tune
"I had my chance,
I let it go."

***

It has become evident
Within our first meeting
That you prided yourself
On being a servant of your Lord.
I could only see it
Because you trusted me
To let me in your heart.

***

Let the magic touch you,
And the words will wrap themselves
around your soul.
Your heart will be coloured with love,
The paint dripping through the organ
And finding its way around your soul.
Your eyes widen like you've seen a
ghost;
It's in fact a realization of something
you've always known.
It's like a breath of fresh air,
And suddenly all of this begins to
make sense.
You smile at your understanding;
Daylight begins.

***

I have seen you in the rays of the sun
As they shine over us;
Enlightening us,
Providing us warmth
On such a cold, cold surface.
And even as the clouds try to block
you out,
You peer through
And you're sight of us is unbreakable
(A comforting fact that cradles us).
If we look hard enough
We could see you.

***

Far away in the distance,
Probably in the darkest hour,
I saw a beacon of light not too far
away.
And it reminded me that,
Even during these dark times,
No matter how foggy the sky or how
weak my eyes,
I will always find a light.

***

I cannot feel it-
The anger of yours you want me to
see.
I can't feel the vicious tongue
That used to cut straight to the bone,
And inflict my nerves with a poisonous
reminder
Ringing like a sharp alarm every now
and then.
Your words have become like text;
Emotionless, meaningless, just a blank
canvas
That once used to bury its meaning in
my mind
And now barely scratches the surface.

And I no longer care.
I want to try, I really do
Yet I feel no remorse.
My only worry surrounds the lack of
that feeling.
I don't know what to say (and I usually
do),
But I think this train is leaving
And I got on it without you.

***

I was walking in the marketplace when I came across a seasoned assassin. I recognized him immediately; his work was famous to anyone who ever existed, distinct like the brush-stroke of an artist. Many had told his stories, and the children had memorized it. However, this man never spoke of his own tales. I always wondered if they were true.

I walked up to him as he was reading a book, and asked him if I could learn the ways of the assassin. He looked at me and his eyes looked empty. He told me that to be an assassin I must learn how to kill. With that, he went back to his book. I looked back at him and told him that anyone could kill, even a child could do it. He shook his head, not picking up his gaze.

Curious and wanting his attention, I asked him how I would go about taking someone's life. He finally took his gaze off his book and looked me in the eye. The empty stare shook me to my core. His eyes were missing something, but I couldn't figure it out. He looked at me and said, "Only those who don't have a soul can take another. When you take a life, you bury yours as well."

I had realized at that very moment
what I found in his eyes; it was
nothing. I walked away, wondering if I
valued life or death more.

***

A four year-old was murdered. His body was found in the middle of the street next to a rock stained in day-old blood, both items cold and lifeless. A man is taken into custody and finds himself in a court amongst the other villagers. The judge asks him if he murdered the child, and the man confesses. Whispers fill the chamber, echoing through and reaching the other side. The judge asks why, and the man explains that his target was not the child but rather his father. The judge turns to the father and asks if he did anything wrong; the father said no. The judge asked the murderer why his wanted to attack the father, and the murderer pointed to another man and laid the blame on him. The other man attacked the murderer the night before. The judge turned to the new man and demanded an explanation. The new man pointed to another man and claimed that the man he was pointing to attacked him. That man pointed his finger to another man in the audience, and that man had a similar response. And the blame went on and on, and the entire town was guilty.

All the while, the little child lay lifeless;
he was the only one in the room not
guilty of any crime.

***

It's at dawn that I come to a realization.
A light that shines past the cliffs, over
the rooftops;
A slow wake-up call.
And as the days pass,
Magic slowly fades into normalcy;
There is no rush, no adrenaline
No excitement that is like a current
jolting through my body.

But it's the mundane
And with you it becomes so beautiful,
Just like how a sunrise may never be
extraordinary
But it is still far from ordinary.

You're a welcome presence.

And it's at dawn where your soft
eyelids slowly open,
And the sun shines as bright as it
always did.
I've never fared well in the dark,
And I've yet to find a storm in your
eyes.

We may have become mundane
But there can never be anything
ordinary with what we have.

***

A young boy sits in a car looking out the window,
Looking at every passenger.
They all seem to look forward, staring at the blackness of the road.
Suddenly he catches the eyes of an older man, face scarred and with a white beard,
And is taken to a whole new world.

Suddenly a life flashes before him, but it's not his.
He sees a life lived, a love lost, and everything in between.
It was scary, to experience a life from a man
He had only seen for a second.

The flashes stopped, and the boy had tears in his eyes.
They rolled down and he held it inside;
He always observed the exteriors and noticed not a thing,
But the interior showed too much when he was brought in.

***

On one side of the world,
A candle is lit in his name;
A wish is whispered,
A prayer is answered.

On another side of the world,
A night is spent with ink
Writings of the treasures of his
surroundings;
A prayer is answered.

On another side of the world,
A stone is set on another;
A home for the divine is built,
A prayer is answered.

And I sit here in observation,
Wondering at these beings.
The same love practiced
In a completely different way.
Is one better, or
Are they all the same?

***

Home is made
With souls,
not words.

***

Foreign words are spoken,
But we hold a familiar language.

I hold her hands
And language is nothing.

***

He focused more on the photographs
Rather than what was behind the
lens--
That was his demise.

***

And suddenly
Now when I imagine my future,
The blank canvas is filled
With your shadow;
I can imagine what it's like
If we spent our lives together;
If we roamed the world or sheltered in
each other,
If I were to see how the seconds pass
When I'm looking in your eyes.

And it may still be a fantasy,
A dream that we have at night,
But the thought remains
When I open my eyes.

***

If you had the help of the one
Who created the skies we look upon
And the sun that keeps us warm
And the ground we find a home,
What says you can't achieve the
world?

***

I was held captive against my own will
But I didn't seem to mind.
Anywhere I turned,
You'd be there
Lying in the context of what
surrounded it.

Simply put, you became everything,
And the clouds would tell me any story
I wanted.
I'd see infinity in your eyes,
I'd found what I really desire;
Doing absolutely nothing with you.
Our souls would move through the
earth;
Taking over the space,
Becoming the air,
Seeping into the ground--
Contaminating every inch with a
reddish hue.

You brought calm to edges of cliffs,
And a tiny speck of light in a dark cave
That was so easy to find.
And the paint would rearrange itself,
Taking over the blank canvas
Becoming you.

I am held captive by my mind
And forced to think of you;
As painful as it may sound,
This is how I'd spend my youth.

***

We've found ourselves in endless
conversation;
Sneaking away, continuing the
discussion.
Just some small jokes and a little
nonsense-
Things that only you and I would ever
get.

But I don't want to stop talking
In fear of you having nothing to
respond to,
Because our words are like kisses
Meeting in the air, a single moment
(One that is so easy to remember).
And when you speak
And look at me
And smile,
It's indescribable.

***

The Stories of the Moon

I looked up on a starry night
When the moon was in sight
And saw a poem written on the surface.
It was fantastical, yet non-fiction,
Of a treasure I had found once before.

It filled me with inspiration & purpose
As I recited it again and again-
But the moon had turned and showed another side,
And the story had reached my memory's end.

All I remember is the moon, not the stories it told
Illuminated by the fires that danced that night.
I have only seen similar stories in the eyes
That meet with me in the morning light.

***

The Traveller: Part II coming soon.

About the Author

Mateen Manek is a writer and poet from Toronto, Canada. He also hosts a politics vlog on YouTube called *Politically Mateen*. He often writes about politics, culture and conflict on his blog *the clearly illiterate cafe*. He has produced four short films and released two musical albums. He also does calligraphy and has an interest in drama, poetry and music.

Mateen is also the co-founder and the creative director of the *30 Nights of Ramadan* project, a website built to feature content surrounding the holy Islamic month of Ramadan. You can visit it by going to http://www.30nightsoframadan.com

You can follow his latest updates on his Twitter (@mateenmanek) or his instagram (@politicallymateen). For all poetry updates, you can follow his poetry account (@mateenmanek) on instagram.

www.ingramcontent.com/pod-product-compliance
Lightning Source LLC
Chambersburg PA
CBHW021942040426
42448CB00008B/1204